Garlic Solutions

A Guide to Choosing, Using and Growing
Nature's Super Food

M.B. Ryther

Disclaimer

This book is not intended as a substitute for the medical advice of physicians. The reader should regularly consult a physician in matters relating to his/her health and particularly with respect to any symptoms that may require diagnosis or medical attention.

Contents

Garlic: Nature's Super Food

"Garlic is as good as ten mothers."

–Chinese proverb

There are few foods that are as widely revered, universally adopted, and as steeped in lore and legend as "the stinking rose," otherwise known as garlic. Its culinary prowess can turn a bland dish into a memorable one, and its health benefits include everything from lowered blood pressure to improved heart health. Some of the most exciting recent medical research links garlic consumption to protection against infection, environmental toxins, and even cancer.

And while its legendary ability to ward off vampires has yet to be proven, it will keep little monsters off your plants, according to the Environmental Protection Agency (EPA), which officially lists garlic as a non-toxic pest control substance. This is just an introduction, for as you'll soon discover, the list of garlic pluses and positives goes on and on.

Which brings us to the purpose of this book: To present to you the wonders of garlic in a simplified, organized, and useful manner so you can start reaping the benefits of this powerful little plant right away. In these pages you'll find tips on how to grow your own garlic, store it, prepare it, eat it, and use it for a variety of purposes, some of which might surprise you. (Fish bait or facial – your choice!)

But first, I'd like to take a short trip back in time to the origins and early uses of this miracle food. What's truly amazing is how imbedded garlic was in the cultures of so many ancient civilizations.

What's also amazing is how in so many instances ancient wisdom has been proven right by modern science.

Garlic Through The Ages

The word "garlic" comes from the Old English word "gar," which means "spear," referring to the plant's spear-shaped leaves. It is widely believed that garlic originated in Central Asia and southwestern Siberia, its cultivation eventually spreading east towards China and west towards Europe.

The ancient Sumerians are credited with the earliest written mention of garlic. A Sumerian clay tablet dating back to 2600 BC named the herb on a list of dietary staples. A thousand years later, in 1550 BC, garlic was prominently featured in the Codex Ebers, a medical text from ancient Egypt. Of the hundreds of herbal remedies mentioned in the text, 22 of them included garlic for the treatment of a variety of medical conditions, including tumors and heart ailments.

We know from artwork and sculptures, papyrus writings, and tomb and temple texts that garlic was highly esteemed in ancient Egypt. It was particularly recognized for its ability to strengthen the body and ward off infection. According to Greek historian Herodotus, the slaves who built the Great Pyramid of Cheops at Giza were given loads of garlic, onions, and radishes to fuel their work. Garlic was so valued it was even used as currency on occasion. A healthy male slave in ancient Egypt could be purchased for fifteen pounds of garlic.

The ancient Greeks also believed in the power of garlic. Greek soldiers ingested it to steel themselves for war. Greek athletes took it to improve their performances in the Olympic games. The famous Greek physician Hippocrates prescribed garlic as a laxative and a diuretic, as well as a treatment for uterine tumors and lung disease. Aristotle wrote of garlic's use as a medicinal remedy, and in particular its usefulness as an aphrodisiac. But as much as the Greeks may have loved garlic for its performance-enhancing and medicinal qualities, they weren't so keen on its smell. In fact, they considered "garlic breath" to be vulgar and offensive. They believed their gods shared this dislike as well, and forbade people from entering select temples if they smelled of garlic. On the other side of the supernatural spectrum, the Greeks held that garlic provided protection from witches, a belief that carried on through subsequent centuries.

Like the Greeks who flourished before them, the ancient Romans also prohibited worshipers from entering their temples after eating garlic. While not popular among the wealthier Romans, who looked down on garlic as a food for peasants and laborers, garlic was highly regarded by Rome's soldiers and sailors, who ingested it abundantly for courage, fortitude, and overall healthfulness. The Romans, like the Greeks, also used garlic for medicinal purposes. In his 37-book encyclopedia of natural sciences, *Historia Naturalis*, Pliny the Elder (23-79 AD) listed 23 different ailments that garlic could be used to treat, including infection, a condition which modern research has shown garlic to be effective against. In another remarkable nod to the future discoveries of modern science, Nero's chief physician, the Greek Dioscorides, wrote in his famous medical text *Meteria Medica* that garlic "clears the arteries and opens the mouths of the veins."

In biblical times, garlic was also highly regarded. Hebrew laborers used it to enhance their strength and health. The one mention of garlic in the Bible, Numbers 11:6, expresses the dissatisfaction among the Israelites, after having been led out of Egypt by Moses, over the lack of garlic and other favored foods: "We remember the fish which we used to eat free in Egypt, the cucumbers and the melons and the leeks and the onions and the garlic . . ." In the Talmud, one of Judaism's core texts, instructions are given for using garlic as a food, medicine, and aphrodisiac.

After the fall of Rome, Christian monks became the chief keepers of herbal and medical knowledge, and consequently grew garlic in their monastery gardens along with other plants considered important and useful. Across Europe, people of all classes began valuing garlic for its medicinal qualities as well as its taste. The Duke of Normandy,

Robert I, in the eleventh century wrote: "Since garlic has the power to save from death, endure it though it gives bad breath." In Germany, the Christian mystic Saint Hildegard von Bingen taught that garlic should be eaten in moderation and that it "ought to be eaten uncooked, because if it is cooked, its strength is lost."

As cultural changes swept across Europe during the fevered years of the Renaissance, garlic rode the wave and stayed afloat, maintaining its renowned stature as a medicinal plant. In 1652, British physician Nicholas Culpeper, in his monumental work *The Complete Herbal*, credited garlic with a plethora of healing powers. A leading Italian physician, Pietro Mattioli of Siena, prescribed garlic for worms, kidney disorders, digestive problems, and to mothers experiencing difficult childbirths.

Perhaps the most interesting use of garlic during these times occurred during the Plague years, when French gravediggers drank crushed garlic in wine to protect themselves from contracting the disease. Similarly, legend has it that thieves who robbed the dead and dying avoided the plague by wearing cotton masks soaked in a mixture of wine vinegar, herbs, and garlic, as well as rubbing the malodorous concoction all over their bodies. And finally, stories from that era maintain that French priests who ministered to plague victims avoided catching it themselves, while English priests were not so lucky. The difference? The French ate lots of garlic; the English, not so much.

The modern era changed garlic's standings significantly. No longer the object of folklore, legends, and anecdotal surmising, garlic began being studied in laboratories and given the scientific validation its supporters through the centuries always knew but couldn't prove. French chemist Louis Pasteur was one of the first modern researchers to observe garlic's potential health benefits. In 1858 he placed some garlic cloves in a petri dish filled with bacteria. When he checked on the dish a few days later, he found that the bacteria had died off. Aware of its antibacterial properties, British doctors during World War I frequently used garlic as an antiseptic against infections. And in World War II, British and Russian doctors used a diluted garlic solution to disinfect open wounds, gaining it the nickname "Russian penicillin."

Today, in addition to being widely popular among consumers, garlic has also attracted the attention of the scientific community. Researchers have conducted numerous studies and produced close to 5,000 scientific articles examining garlic's health effects. While not every therapeutic claim made through the centuries has been proven, garlic has earned the distinction of being included in a group of foods known as "nutriceuticals," that is, foods that are known to provide health benefits beyond basic nutrition. Flax, oats, soy, tomatoes, cruciferous vegetables, and citrus fruits are also nutraceuticals.

Garlic Basics

Garlic is a member of the *Alliaceae* family, or lily family, of the plant genus *Allium*, which includes onions, leeks, shallots, chives, and garlic. Garlic plants have long, flat, spear-shaped leaves that typically grow between 16 and 18 inches tall. The garlic bulb itself consists of anywhere from three to forty cloves, and inside each clove is a bud that can produce a new plant.

There are two main subspecies of garlic: hardneck and softneck. Hardneck garlic produces long, curly stalks called "scapes" that in turn will produce little bulblets at their ends. The scapes start to appear a month or so after the first leaves, and are usually cut off by growers to encourage growth of the larger bulb. Softneck garlic does not produce scapes, but does produce larger bulbs and more cloves per bulb. Softneck is easier to grow and keeps longer than its hardneck cousin. For all of these reasons, it is the variety most often seen in grocery stores.

The often talked-about elephant garlic is actually not a garlic plant at all, but rather a leek. But because it so closely smells like garlic and looks like garlic (albeit in a gigantic sense – some elephant bulbs can weigh as much as a pound!), many people mistake it for just a bigger variety of the stinking rose. And for many people, especially those who prefer a milder garlic taste, elephant garlic is a suitable substitute for the real thing.

Garlic can be grown in a wide sphere of climates and landscape. Gilroy, California, is famously known as the "Garlic Capital of the World," and for good reason: it is the largest garlic producer in the United States and is home to the renowned Gilroy Garlic Festival, which has been held annually since 1979 and has grown into one of the largest food festivals anywhere. China, however, holds the title of the world's largest garlic producer, and accounts for approximately two-thirds of the global garlic output.

It is now known that garlic contains over 200 chemical compounds that work together to make it a nutritional wonder. Those compounds include vitamins, minerals, amino acids, enzymes, and numerous sulfur compounds. When garlic is crushed, cut, or eaten, it produces allicin, one of the most biologically active compounds in garlic and the one that gives the stinking rose its distinctive odor. Allicin also is the compound that gives garlic its greatest reputed health benefits, as it has been proven to contain antibacterial, antifungal, antiviral, and antioxidant properties.

Researchers are still trying to figure out all of garlic's biochemical mysteries, but in the meantime, never forget that regardless of whether you think of garlic as a vegetable, condiment, spice, herb, medicine, or supplement – or all of the above – it is first and foremost a great-tasting food. So eat and enjoy!

Choosing and Buying

"I can't get enough garlic!"

–Ted Williams

So, how do you like your garlic? Raw, whole, crushed, minced, chopped, pureed, powdered, or as a pill – consumers have more choices than ever when it comes to buying garlic. Even more mind-boggling is the number of garlic products available in today's marketplace – everything from garlic salsas and garlic mustards to pickled garlic and garlic-flavored hot sauces (in varying degrees of intensity, of course!).

To demystify the choosing and purchasing process, let's start with some simple explanations of the different forms of garlic. Once you know what's available and what it's best used for, you'll be better able to choose the best garlic for your tastes and purposes.

Fresh

Garlic in its purest form. Plucked from your own garden or bought from a local grocer, raw bulbs of garlic provide the most versatility and the strongest flavor. You can eat them as is (i.e., raw, in which case the health benefits are believed to be strongest), cook them whole, chop them up, add them to recipes, or tie them into braids for a unique wall hanging. Straight from the ground, raw garlic will last up to six months if stored in a cool, dry place. If you've bought your garlic from a grocery store, you have no idea how long it's been on the store shelves, so don't count on the same freshness span.

Keep these tips in mind when shopping for fresh garlic:

- Avoid buying garlic from May through mid-July. Last year's summer crop is pretty well gone by then, and it's too early for the new harvest. Also, out-of-season garlic may have been treated with sprout inhibitors or irradiation to keep longer.

- Look for firm, heavy, blemish-free bulbs with tight skins. Press the outer cloves with your fingers. If they're not firm and solid, the garlic is old and beginning to deteriorate.

- Softneck varieties are more common in grocery stores. Hardneck varieties (the choice of many garlic connoisseurs) may have to be purchased at farmers markets and specialty stores. You can tell the difference by looking for the hard core that comes out the center of a hardneck bulb to form the stem.

- Consider buying organically grown garlic if it's available in your area. Not only will you financially help smaller family farms, you'll get garlic that has few to none harmful pesticides on it, a higher content of phytonutrients, and overall more nutritional content.

Crushed, Minced and Chopped

Jars of pre-prepped garlic are ideal for the both the casual and more serious cook. While garlic aficionados might be apt to dismiss "jarred garlic" as an inferior choice for quality and taste, most people aren't going to notice a difference. And for convenience, jarred garlic is hard to beat. The only prep work involved is opening the bottle and spooning some out. Once opened, a jar of garlic should last up to three months in the refrigerator with no discernable diminishment in flavor. The other advantage to having jarred garlic around? You'll be more inclined to use it!

Whether you prep the garlic yourself or get it from a jar, be aware of these differences in flavor and aroma:

- **Crushed:** Will provide the strongest flavor and aroma. Crushing fresh, raw garlic breaks down the cell walls and releases the most allicin; hence the most aroma and flavor. Great for dishes like garlic bread where you really want to taste the garlic and not much else, as it will overpower other flavors.

- **Minced:** Not as intense. Better used in recipes such as stir fry dishes where you want the garlic to play nice with other flavors.

- **Chopped:** Least pungent. Best used in dishes where you want a little garlic flavoring. Easy to remove from a dish, too, after it's lent its flavoring to the mix.

As a general rule, remember: The smaller the cut and the less the cooking time, the stronger the taste.

Dehydrated

Approximately 75 percent of all garlic grown in the United States is used for dehydrated garlic products. It is planted specifically for high yield and is processed by three or four large firms. Dehydrated garlic is used mainly in processed foods (read the ingredients list on your pantry items and see for yourself!), but another large portion is used to make garlic granules, garlic powder, garlic salt, and other garlic seasonings.

As in the case of jarred garlic, "powdered garlic" and its ilk is a poor second cousin to fresh garlic in the minds of many garlic enthusiasts. Nonetheless, many of these products are a staple in most people's spice cabinets and come in very handy when you're in a hurry, when you need a dash of garlic in a recipe, or you just want to sprinkle something "garlicky" on your veggies.

- **Granulated garlic** is best used when you want a strong garlic flavor without the hassle and mess of mincing fresh garlic. It has a grainy texture like fine cornmeal. It is great in sauces and dry rubs, where it blends in easily.

- **Garlic powder** is easier to find in grocery stores and can be used interchangeably with granulated garlic. It has a finer, flour-like consistency. In its purest form, garlic powder is simply dehydrated garlic cloves ground into a powder. Some brands contain additives to supposedly "enhance" the color and/or flavor. Check the label to know what you're buying. Garlic powder mixes well in liquids, making it a good choice for marinades and sauces.

- **Garlic salt** is a food seasoning made by combining salt and garlic powder. Commercial brands often include in the mix an anti-clumping agent such as calcium silicate. Because it contains less salt than regular table salt, it's a great alternative for those watching their sodium intake. To make your own garlic salt, simply mix three parts salt to one part garlic powder and store in an airtight container.

Freeze-Dried Garlic

Another popular form of dehydrated garlic, especially amongst survivalists, is freeze-dried garlic. This is fresh garlic that has been frozen and had the water removed. It reconstitutes quickly in a little bit of liquid (even your saliva is enough to kick in the taste if you put a piece in your mouth). When used in cooking, especially in savory dishes such as stews, the garlicky flavor is surprisingly strong. As an added bonus, it doesn't have to be stored in the refrigerator, which makes it handy for campers, "preppers," and those awaiting the zombie apocalypse.

Garlic Juice

Garlic juice is just what it sounds like, the pungent liquid squeezed from garlic cloves. While you could make your own with a blender, commercially it is usually sold in spray cans for easy, convenient use. A typical 8 oz. can contains juice from approximately 150 cloves and is good for supposedly 1,000 sprays. Garlic juice spray is a great way to add garlic flavoring to pasta, potatoes, sandwiches, salads, meats, pizza, and more.

Many gardeners use garlic spray to keep pests away. It doesn't kill the beneficial bugs (or pose health risks to people and pets), but its pungent odor does makes plants undesirable as a place to eat or nest.

True garlic lovers may even want to spritz it on as a perfume!

Garlic Oil

Garlic oils were the first commercially-processed garlic product, going back about 80 years. They are made in two different ways. The first uses high temperatures to "steam distill" crushed garlic. Oil is released and captured during this process as allicin breaks down into sulfides. Because it takes about a pound of garlic to produce a gram of oil, vegetable oil is added to the garlic oil that goes into the capsules you see on store shelves. This diluted form of garlic oil is still very beneficial, as it contains oil-soluble sulfides that studies have shown to circulate via the lymphatic system, enhancing the immune system and acting in an antibacterial manner.

The second way garlic oil is prepared is by soaking macerated (chopped or crushed) garlic in vegetable oil for 24 hours and then straining out the chunks of garlic. While garlic macerate oil contains lesser amounts of fat-soluble polysulfides than steam-distilled garlic oil, it contains higher amounts of water-soluble compounds that circulate throughout the blood stream, thus producing benefits to the heart and circulatory system. It also contains ajoene, a compound that forms when allicin is dissolved in various solvents such as oil.

Ajoene has been proven to have strong anticlotting, antibacterial and antifungal properties.

If taking garlic oil capsules for health reasons, both types should be taken if possible, since they contain different healthful compounds. Macerate oil is more commonly found in Europe than in the United States, however, and may have to be mail-ordered.

Garlic oil pills can also be used in cooking. Simply cut them open and add to stews, soups, sauces, and salad dressings for a pinch of garlic-infused flavor.

> ***Important Note:*** *Making your own garlic oil at home could be risky. If left unrefrigerated or kept too long, the very real threat of botulism can occur. The FDA recommends using homemade oil right away after making it. If saving leftovers, refrigerate and discard after a week. Commercially-prepared garlic oils usually contain a preservative or acid, which preserves the garlic and protects it from growing harmful bacteria.*

Garlic Powder Capsules and Pills

Garlic pills, tablets, and capsules are nothing more than garlic powder inserted into a gelatin or vegetarian capsule or pressed into a pill. Although the consumer does get a measured dose of garlic, the quality of the garlic can't always be assured. The amount of allicin that will be formed when the garlic hits the digestive system is dependent on the variety of garlic used to make the powder and the manner in which the powder was made. One trick to use when taking garlic powder pills is to drink one full glass of water at the same time. The water will dilute the stomach acid sufficiently for the garlic powder to mix with the water and form allicin. The allicin-containing water then leaves the stomach through tiny capillaries in the stomach's walls, where the allicin enters into the bloodstream and is further broken down and used by the body.

Many people prefer reduced odor enteric-coated garlic pills, not only because of the promise of less "garlic breath," but also because of the claim that they can pass through the stomach intact and not dissolve until they get to the duodenum, where the less acidic intestinal fluids mix with the garlic powder to produce a good shot of allicin and other compounds which then are dispersed into the user's system. In theory, they work great, but only if the enteric coating works properly. If it dissolves too soon, stomach acid will neutralize much of the formation of allicin. If it dissolves too late, the pill could pass through the user's system largely undigested and with no benefit at all. To be on the safe side, buy from a reputable manufacturer that guarantees their pill's potency.

In 1994, Dr. Larry Lawson, author of the book, *Garlic: The Science and Therapeutic Application of Allium Sativum L. and Related Species*, conducted a study of 28 types of garlic pills to see which ones produced the most allicin in the body. Not too surprisingly, the study showed that the enteric-coated pills – if they dissolved correctly – produced the highest levels of allicin. For legal reasons, he couldn't say which brands did best, but there is a simple way to know if the garlic pill you took is producing results. A few hours after ingesting it, you should be able to detect a secondary garlic odor emanating from you, even if very faint. As Dr. Paul Wargovich of Houston's M.D. Anderson Cancer Center once said, "If it doesn't stink, it doesn't work."

Aged Garlic Extract

One type of garlic product that is guaranteed not to stink, because it purposely doesn't contain any allicin, is aged garlic extract (AGE). Known by its brand name Kyolic, AGE is at the complete opposite end of the garlic supplement spectrum. Whereas most other supplement makers tout allicin as the healthful by-product of garlic, Kyolic believes that allicin is not the shining star its proponents claim. In fact, AGE's supporters claim that most top garlic products contain only negligible amounts of allicin at best, and even if they produced as much as claimed, it's a moot point because allicin is not biologically active in the body. Kyolic argues that their garlic supplement, which is made by chopping garlic and aging it for 20 months in an ethanol solution, contains milder, less odorous, and more health-promoting compounds, including the amino acids S-allyl cysteine and S-allyl mercaptocysteine.

One of AGE's biggest cheerleaders is Dr. Matthew Budoff, a cardiologist and professor of medicine at UCLA. Dr. Budoff has conducted numerous studies on the effectiveness of aged garlic extract on cardiovascular health. The results of those studies, published in major academic journals, consistently show that aged garlic extract lowers blood pressure, reduces blood clotting, and drops cholesterol and triglyceride levels. "I think aged garlic extract should be taken right alongside your multivitamins every day. It's that important," says Budoff. "It could save your life." Dr. Budoff recommends 1,200 mg. of aged garlic extract daily as a health supplement.

For people interested in taking garlic supplements for health, perhaps the answer is to take both types: allicin-based for its anti-tumor and immune-enhancing properties, and AGE for circulatory system health.

Growing and Storing

"There is no such thing as a little garlic."

–Arthur Baer

Anyone can grow garlic. It's one of the easiest plants to grow, requires relatively little care once planted (especially if you plant softneck garlic), is fun and rewarding to harvest, and best of all, it tastes great. In fact, once you experience garlic from your own garden, you won't ever want to go back to supermarket garlic again! Here are some easy-to-follow guidelines that will have you reaping (and reeking) in no time.

Planting

- Decide what type of garlic you're going to plant. As a general rule, hardneck garlic does best in Northern climates and softneck varieties do better in the South. For optimal results, check with local growers, a gardening association, or extension service to determine the best type of garlic to plant.

- Plant garlic cloves in late September to mid-October. In places like the deep South where the ground typically doesn't freeze, you can plant as late as December or January.

- Spring planting is generally not recommended, as garlic ideally requires about 9 months gestation time. But if you don't mind "green" or immature garlic – and many cooks and aficionados not only don't mind it, but love it – then plant without worry. The resulting plant will resemble a scallion with a deep green stalk and a pale white bulb.

- Use bulbs that are large and firm. Make sure there are no soft spots or mildew on the cloves.

- Divide the bulbs into cloves only when ready to plant; early separation lessens yield. (Garlic does not produce fertile seeds, so it is propagated using the cloves. Each clove contains a bud with the potential to yield a new plant.)

- Use only the largest and best-looking cloves for planting. There's no need to peel the cloves.

- Beware of using supermarket garlic for planting. It is often specially treated so as not to sprout. Also, it may have been imported from a region not suitable for your climate.

- Plant in a sunny location.

- Plant in crumbly, light soil that drains well and that is high in organic matter. (If you live in an area that gets a lot of rain, consider using raised beds for better drainage.)

- Plant cloves 2 to 4 inches down, 6 to 8 inches apart, pointy sides up. Space rows 12 inches to 18 inches apart.

Cultivating

- Mulch with several inches of leaves or straw to protect the cloves over the winter months.

- Weed often to prevent cloves from losing light and nutrients.

- Watch for the emergence of scapes (the green curling stalks that contain tiny bulblets) around mid-June if you've planted hardneck garlic. These should be cut off as soon as they appear to encourage growth of the larger garlic bulb. Both the stalks and bulblets are edible, and are delicious sautéed or steamed.

- Fertilize fall-planted garlic in early spring, and spring-planted garlic in early summer. Avoid "burning" by placing the fertilizer four to six inches on either side of the bulb. Fine compost, manure tea and balanced liquid fertilizers all work well.

- Keep the beds evenly moist. Be careful not to overwater, which can result in the growth of crop-damaging fungus. Stop watering two weeks before harvesting or when tops begin to dry to let the bulbs mature. This will generally happen some time in July.

Harvesting

- The bulbs are ready to harvest when the majority of the leaves have turned yellow and dry but there are still three or four green leaves left on each plant. Waiting too much longer increases the occurrence of split skins and broken bulbs. Typically garlic is ready to harvest between the first week of July to mid-August, depending on the strain, climate, and location.

- Using a digging fork, carefully loosen the soil and lift the plants out. Do not pull the tops. The skin around the bulbs should be thick, dry, and paper-like. (Discard any bruised or damaged bulbs; they can't be stored.)

- Treat the garlic like eggs. It's very fragile and can bruise easily. Even the smallest bump can cause early decay and loss of quality.

- Shake off loose dirt and allow bulbs to dry on a wooden or wire rack or on a cloth screen.

- Keep the garlic out of direct sunlight to prevent "cooking." A cool, dry, well-ventilated shed or garage is a good place for this curing phase.

- Allow the bulbs to dry for about two weeks, or until the outer skin is papery. Then trim the tops and the roots to within an inch of the bulbs.

Storing

- Store the bulbs in a cool, dry place with good ventilation. Hanging baskets, mesh bags, old pantyhose, cardboard boxes, or clay pots with holes are all good storage containers. The garlic will keep for six to eight months.

- Resist the urge to clean the bulbs too much before storing them. Wait until you're ready to use the garlic and then clean it thoroughly. Otherwise you run the risk of shortening its shelf life due to excessive handling and/or bruising.

- Keep stored garlic away from foods that might absorb its flavor, such as potatoes or fruit.

- Braiding garlic is not only a convenient way to store the bulbs, but it can also be a lucrative side venture. Braided garlic can sell for double the price per pound of loose garlic.

- Pigtail braiding works best with softneck garlic because of its more pliable stalk, and should be done before the tops are completely dried. Be sure to use clean and "pretty" bulbs, especially if you plan on selling the braids, giving them as gifts, or hanging them in your kitchen as functional accent pieces.

- There is a bit of a learning curve to braiding garlic, and some people learn better by watching live demonstrations or videos than they do reading about it. If you fall into this category, try searching on YouTube for "how to braid garlic" videos. For a particularly good textual explanation (with photos), visit the WikiHow.com page on "How to Braid Garlic." (www.wikihow.com/Braid-Garlic)

- If you have neither the patience nor inclination to try your hand at braiding, you can "faux braid." Make a bundle of three or more bulbs and tie them together with string, twine, floral wire, or zip ties.

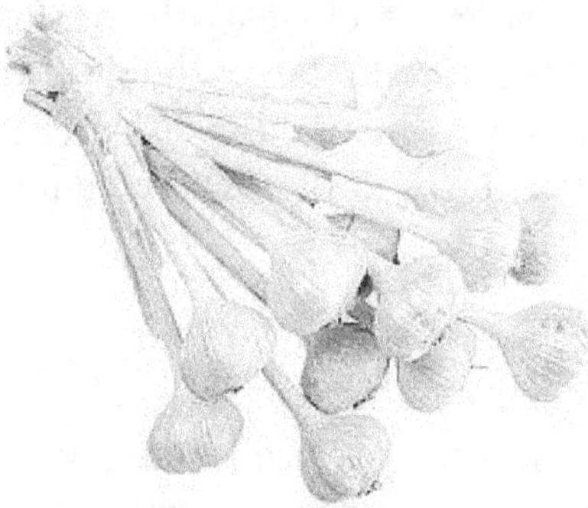

- Finished braids and bundles can be decorated with dried grasses, flowers, herbs, ribbons, and bows. Some people mix peppers and onions into the bunch. How about adding a decorative label with a recipe written on it? Be as creative as you like.

- In folklore, and even in certain communities today, braided garlic is believed to protect the house in which it hangs from ghosts, spirits, and negative energy that may be lurking about.

For Fun

- **Garlic Barrels** – Garlic can easily be grown in large containers such as wine barrels. Let your children create their own "garlic garden" in one of these by planting cloves around the perimeter of the barrel in the fall and then, in the spring, planting flowers in the middle to complement the growing garlic.

- **Garlic Pots** – On an even smaller scale, you can grow green garlic (garlic grass) in a flowerpot right on your windowsill or patio. (Green garlic is immature garlic that has been planted too close together to grow to full size.) Simply take several unpeeled cloves and plant them about one inch deep in a pot filled with good quality potting soil. Water the garlic and set the pot in a sunny location. Keep the soil moist but don't overwater or the cloves will rot. In about three weeks you should have sprouts large enough to snip and use as in cooking and as a garlicky garnish. After about three months, when the grass ceases to flourish, replant and start over.

Extra Planting Tips

- Garlic and roses make visually attractive companion plants. Additionally, many gardeners believe that planting garlic with roses enhances their scent and helps keep the flowers free of diseases and pests.

- Planting garlic around the base of fruit trees is believed by many growers to repel borers and aphids. It is also believed by some to keep rabbits and other hungry critters out of the garden.

- Don't plant garlic close to peas, potatoes, beans and other legumes. It could have an adverse effect on those crops' growth and flavor.

- Don't plant garlic where onions were previously planted. The soil could be contaminated with pests or diseases.

Cooking With Garlic

"No cook who has attained mastery over her craft ever apologizes for the presence of garlic in her productions."

–Ruth Gottfried, *The Questing Cook* (1927)

There are as many different ways to cook with garlic as there are varieties of garlic and types of cooks. If your experience with garlic is limited to sprinkling a little garlic powder on your green beans, these tips and hints will turn you from a neophyte to a natural in no time. And if you're already a garlic *amant*, you might still learn a new thing or two.

Prepping

Whenever possible, use fresh garlic. Not only is the flavor better, but commercially processed garlic products, while useful from time to time, can sometimes contain less than 20 percent actual garlic due to the addition of added salts and anti-caking agents. However, if you do resort to using fresh garlic alternatives, here are some handy measurement guides:

Garlic Product Equivalents of 1 Clove:

1 teaspoon of chopped

$^1/_2$ teaspoon of minced garlic

$^1/_8$ teaspoon of garlic powder

$^1/_4$ teaspoon of garlic juice

$^1/_2$ teaspoon of garlic salt (omit $^1/_2$ teaspoon of regular salt from recipe)

When following recipes, don't over-garlic things by mistaking a bulb for a clove. Remember: The cloves are the small individual segments contained within a bulb of garlic.

To peel garlic, place a clove on a cutting board, place a wide-bladed knife across the top, then whack the flat surface of the knife with the palm of your hand. This should loosen the skin and make for easy peeling.

To chop garlic, cut the clove in half lengthwise. Remove the bitter green core if there is one. Make several more lengthwise cuts, then cut crosswise.

To crush garlic by hand, lay the flat side of a wide-bladed knife over the peeled clove and smash again with the heel of your hand.

To mince garlic by hand, first crush it, then chop it roughly. Next, mince it into fine little pieces using a rocking motion with the edge of your knife. (Keep the tip of the knife on the cutting board and move the handle up and down for a controlled, fluid motion.)

The more you mash, mince, slice and dice garlic, the stronger the flavor (and smell), due to the release of allicin.

Invest in a good quality garlic press. Cheap ones break easily, are difficult to clean, and require a lot of hand strength.

Pressed garlic is generally more flavorful than minced or chopped.

Cooking

Cooking garlic decreases the strength of its flavor. The allicin that is produced when garlic is crushed or chopped transforms into something much milder when exposed to prolonged heat. In fact, if you cook cloves of garlic whole, they won't produce allicin at all.

That's not to say, though, that allicin won't be released when crushed with your teeth! So if you don't want that "complete" garlic experience, avoid biting into those large chunks.

But if you like your garlic wild, not mild, simply press /crush /chop it and add it to your dish in all its glorious raw beauty without cooking it, or at the very end of your dish's cooking time.

As just discussed, the longer garlic is cooked, the milder and sweeter it will be. Different degrees of garlic strength are also achieved by how it's cut, the size of the pieces, the type of garlic used, and the cooking method.

Roasting garlic imparts to it a nutty, almost caramelized, flavor.

If sautéeing, consider cutting the garlic into matchsticks rather than mincing. This will help prevent burning.

When sautéeing garlic and onions together, be sure to start the onions first and let them cook for about half their cooking time. Garlic doesn't take as long, and if overcooked it releases a chemical that will turn your flavors bitter.

When cooking garlic in a microwave, increase the amount you'd normally use by a little bit, as this method of cooking decreases its potency.

For a mild garlic taste in a dish, spear a clove of garlic with a fork and stir it around in the dish. Discard the clove when done.

Remedy a soup or stew to which too much garlic has been added by simmering a small quantity of parsley in it for about 10 minutes.

Cleanup

Store fresh garlic heads in a cool, dry place like your pantry. Don't put them in the refrigerator or they'll start to sprout and turn bitter.

To store individual cloves, simply peel them and keep them in the freezer in freezer bags. When thawed, the cloves may be a little mushy but will still have their flavor.

You can also freeze prepared garlic. Press, crush, or mince the cloves, mix with a little water and freeze them in ice cube trays. You can also mix with olive oil and freeze, or simply freeze the prepared cloves by themselves.

> *Do not store garlic in oil at room temperature! The very real risk of botulism spores developing exists in this condition.*

Plant several bulblets in a flowerpot and keep it in your kitchen for fresh seasonings.

Remove garlic odor from your hands by rubbing your hands on stainless steel (spoon, sink, etc.) under running water.

Remove garlic smell from cutting boards and other surfaces with these tricks: scrub with a paste of baking soda and water; rinse with lemon juice or vinegar; wipe down with a cut tomato or a large strawberry. (If you plan on working a lot with garlic, you may want to dedicate a cutting board just for it.)

Make A Garlic Vinegar

Simply add whole cloves or chopped garlic to a bottle of white or red wine vinegar. How much you add is up to your individual taste; just make sure the garlic is completely submerged. Non-refrigerated vinegar should last about two to three months if kept in a cool, dark place. Refrigerated, it will last about four to six months. Discard if mold develops, or if it develops a bubbly, cloudy or slimy appearance, which is an indication of yeast growth.

Make A Garlic Paste

Good for those who don't like chunks of garlic or when an even distribution of garlic is needed in a dish. First, slice cloves, mince, and sprinkle with salt. Second, mash by pulling an angled chef's knife across the garlic. The salt will extract the moisture and the resultant paste can then be used to impart a uniform garlic flavor in any number of dishes.

Eat The Scapes!

Garlic leaves and flowers (scapes) are very edible, and are considered a delicacy in some parts of the world, particularly Korea and China. They have a mild garlic flavor that lends them to a variety of uses, much like scallions and chives. The are especially good in pesto, and can also be added raw to salads, dips and spreads, or used as a garnish. Chopped and cooked, scapes are great in stir fry, rice, frittatas, soups, stews, and marinades. They can also be eaten alone; try sautéeing them in butter or olive oil along with a little salt and pepper for a delicious sidedish.

The Simple Way To Roast Garlic

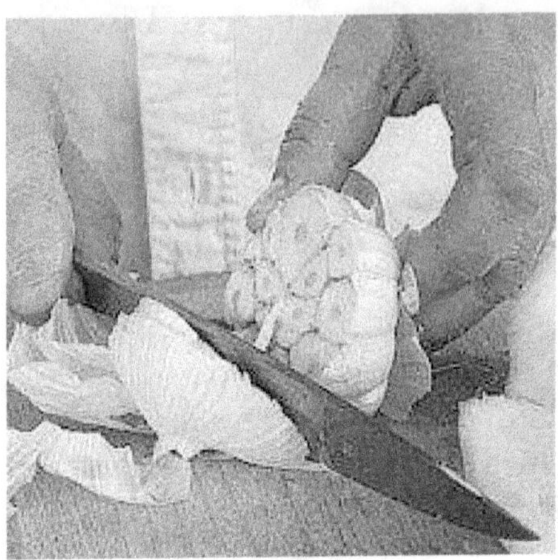

Take a head of garlic and slice off about a quarter-inch from the top.

Repeat with as many heads as you like.

Place in a shallow baking pan, exposed cloves up.

Drizzle with olive oil.

Cover the pan tightly with aluminum foil.

Roast in a 350 degree oven for 30-45 minutes, or until lightly browned and soft. (If cooking in a terracotta roaster, increase cooking time by about 15 minutes.)

You can pop the cloves out with either the tip of a paring knife or by simply squeezing them out of their wrappers.

What To Do With Roasted Garlic

Many people like to eat the roasted garlic just as it is: warm, soft and yummy. But there are endless other possibilities. Here are just a few:

- Add it to soups and stews

- Stir it into gravies, sauces and salsas

- Mix it into dips and spreads

- Spread it on bread alone or topped with mozzarella

- Mix it into mashed potatoes

- Serve it over baked potatoes (mix with a little sour cream, if you like)

- Mix it with butter and spread it over corn-on-the-cob, or any other vegetable for that matter

- Use as a topping for crackers

- Combine with a little olive oil and toss with pasta

- Spread on pizza dough before adding other layers

- Mix into cooked rice and beans

- Add to scrambled eggs, omelets and frittatas

- Try as a condiment on hot dogs, hamburgers and sandwiches

Of course, any of these ideas can also be done with other garlic products (powders, salts, jarred). Adjust the amounts according to your taste.

Make A Garlic Spread

Take the outer layers of skin off a garlic bulb. Pull apart the cloves and place them on a piece of aluminum foil big enough to encase the cloves. Drizzle the cloves with a teaspoon of olive oil. Pull up the corners of the tin foil to loosely envelope the cloves, then pinch closed all openings. Roast in a 350 degree oven for 30 minutes, or until the cloves are soft. Spread it on potatoes, other vegetables, or French bread for a savory delight.

Easy 5–Star Garlic Bread

Ingredients

4 cloves garlic, crushed (or 1/2 teaspoon of garlic powder)

2 tablespoons butter

2 tablespoons extra-virgin olive oil

1 loaf of French bread, split lengthwise

3 tablespoons grated Parmesan or Romano cheese (optional)

Chopped fresh parsley

Directions

Combine garlic, butter, and oil in a small saucepan and heat over moderate-low heat for 3 minutes. (Don't allow to burn.)

Place bread on broiler pan and toast under broiler until golden brown. Brush bread with a generous amount of the heated garlic oil. Sprinkle with cheese (optional) and parsley. If you added cheese, return to broiler and brown for an additional 30 seconds. Cut into pieces and serve.

Quick and Easy Garlic Butter

1/2 pound of butter (2 sticks)

12 cloves of garlic, pressed or crushed

1/4 finely chopped fresh parsley

Pinch of salt (optional)

Combine all ingredients in a large bowl. Then on a sheet of wax paper, shape the mixture into a log. Slice off what you need for buttering bread, vegetables, etc. Keep in refrigerator for no longer than two weeks. For long term storage, wrap in wax paper, place in a freezer bag, and keep in the freezer.

Now that you've got the hang of cooking with garlic, try out any of the thousands of garlic-infused recipes found on the internet or in cookbooks. Chances are you'll approach them with a whole new appreciation of their star ingredient.

Garlic and Health

Garlic with May butter
Cureth all disease.
Drink of goat's white milk
Take along with these.

–Irish proverb

Garlic has been hailed through the centuries as an herbal "wonder drug," having been used at one time or another to treat everything from the common cold to bubonic plague. Unlike so many other "miracles" from bygone eras, garlic's medicinal reputation has actually achieved respectability in the modern age due to scads of scientific research. As Pat Kendall, a PhD food science and nutrition specialist from Colorado State University, succinctly states: "Although [garlic] remedies sound like folklore, modern science provides evidence to back up garlic's claim to fame."

Indeed, nearly 5,000 medical, pharmacological, chemical, and assorted other studies have distinguished garlic as the most studied herb on the planet. While many of these studies resulted in inconclusive and, in some cases, conflicting evidence of garlic's prowess, a great many of them – too many to be ignored – proved exactly the opposite: that garlic is a powerful, effective agent in the treatment of and prevention against many health conditions.

While scientists can't pinpoint any one factor explaining garlic's health benefits, it is widely agreed that the "stinking rose" is a complex, integrated substance that still needs much study to fully understand why and how it does what it does. Here's what we do know so far, summarized aptly by Dr. Steven Pratt in his book *Superfoods Healthstyle:*

"Garlic's power as a heath promoter comes from its rich variety of sulfur containing compounds. Of the nearly one hundred nutrients in garlic, the most important in terms of health benefits seems to be the sulfur compound allicin—an amino acid. Allicin is not present in fresh garlic, but it is formed instantly when cloves are crushed, chewed, or cut. Allicin seems to be responsible for the superbiological activity of garlic as well as its odor. In addition to allicin, a single clove of garlic offers a stew of compounds with potential health benefits, including saponins, phosphorus, potassium, zinc, selenium, polyphenols, and arginine. In addition to these compounds, garlic is a good source of vitamin B6 and also of vitamin C. As with most whole foods, garlic's antioxidant and anti-inflammatory abilities are probably due to the sum of the whole rather than a single agent."

Listed below are the major health conditions that garlic is believed to have an impact on. As with any discussion of alternative health remedies, this information is presented with the understanding that the reader will exercise caution and common sense in making any health decisions based solely on this data.

Cardiovascular Health

Cholesterol

A number of studies done in the 1980s showed that garlic can lower total cholesterol and especially the "bad" type of cholesterol, LDL. These studies have since been criticized as being poorly designed and thus producing unreliable data. Particularly challenging to these earlier findings was a 2007 study led by Stanford professor Christopher Gardner. In this study published in the *Archives of*

Internal Medicine, 192 participants ingested one clove of garlic a day (in either raw or supplement form) for six months. At the end of the trial, virtually no effect on cholesterol was detected in any of the subjects.

While the Gardner study is looked at by many as "ending the discussion" on garlic and its effects on cholesterol, research still continues – and often with results that muddy the water further. For example, a 2012 study conducted by researchers at the Institute of Toxicology at Shandong University in China found that garlic did indeed reduce cholesterol and triglyceride levels in its subjects, and concluded that "garlic therapy should benefit patients with risk of cardiovascular diseases."

Another study that supports garlic's cholesterol-lowering abilities was published in the *Journal of the Royal College of Physicians* in 1994, wherein it showed garlic supplements to lower total serum cholesterol levels by 12 percent after only four weeks of treatment. Even more impressively, LDL levels were lowered by 4 to 15 percent, while HDL (the "good" cholesterol) levels were either left untouched or were raised, some by as much as 22 percent. Triglyceride levels were also lowered in this meta-analysis.

Perhaps the wisest commentary on this divisive topic was given by Dr. Benjamin Lau, author of the book *Garlic and You*. Dr. Lau, a professor of microbiology, immunology, and surgery at Loma Linda University, conducted his own clinical trials with aged garlic extract and found that cholesterol levels did improve, but only after several months of supplementation. He believes this was due to the time it took for the garlic to move the fats from the tissues to the blood, where they were then broken down and excreted through the intestinal tract. Even though his trial was a success overall, there were a few participants who did not respond to the garlic therapy. These folks were found to have the worst diets in terms of high sugar content, processed carbohydrates, and fatty meats. After they cleaned up their diets, the garlic supplementation lowered their lipid levels as well. Dr. Lau's conclusion? Garlic is most effective when used in unison with a healthful diet.

Blood Pressure

Studies consistently conclude that taking regular doses of garlic can lower a person's blood pressure by as much as 7% to 8%. Note that this doesn't mean it can *cure* hypertension, but it can definitely help. And it's also important to remember that it's not as fast-acting as high blood pressure medication.

One of the most recent studies comes from the University of Adelaide in South Australia. In 2012, 80 participants were given either aged garlic extract or a placebo. At the end of the 12-week trial, the garlic extract group experienced a reduction in systolic blood pressure of about 12 mmHg. The study was published in the *European Journal of Clinical Nutrition* and concluded that a daily dose of two pills containing high-potency aged garlic extract seems to help lower blood pressure.

Even more interesting, according to the study's director, Karin Ried, was the effect the garlic had on patients who previously had trouble lowering their blood pressure even with medicine. "What's exciting is that the garlic was able to reduce blood pressure in that medication-resistant group," said Ried, as reported by Australian newspaper *The Age*.

Scientists believe that garlic helps to lower high blood pressure by stimulating the production of naturally occurring chemicals in the body like hydrogen sulfide and nitric oxide, which expand and relax blood vessels and thus ease blood flow.

Blood Clots and Plaque Buildup

The third crucial role garlic plays in cardiovascular health is its abilities to prevent blood clots and reduce artery plaque buildup. The chemical compound in garlic known as ajoene (formed when two allicin molecules react) decreases the stickiness of blood platelets, thereby lessening the possibility of their forming clumps that adhere to artery walls. This is important, of course, as many heart attacks and strokes are believed to be caused by spontaneous clots in the blood vessels.

The usual cause of heart attacks, strokes, and peripheral arterial disease, however, is the growth of cholesterol plaques that over time can block arteries and place blood flow at risk. Exciting new research suggests that garlic may be effective in fighting the growth of plaque, and possibly even reducing pre-existing plaque buildup.

In a study reported by Science Daily News in January 2016, researchers at LA BioMed found significant plaque reduction in the arteries of patients with metabolic syndrome who took aged garlic extract (AGE). Metabolic syndrome is characterized by obesity, high blood pressure, and other cardiac risk factors.

The year-long study involved 55 adult participants who had been diagnosed with metabolic syndrome. At the beginning of the study, the participants' levels of artery plaque buildup and calcium deposits were measured by means of advanced imaging technology. Then the participants were given either a placebo or 2,400 milligrams of aged garlic extract every day. At the end of a year, the participants were retested using the same imaging process. Those who had taken the AGE showed a slowing of total plaque accumulation by 80%. Moreover, the garlic takers showed a reduction of soft plaque and a regression (less plaque on follow-up) of low-attenuation plaque.

Lead researcher Dr. Matthew Budoff lauded these findings in his statement: "We have completed four randomized studies, and they have led us to conclude that Aged Garlic Extract can help slow the progression of atherosclerosis and reverse the early stages of heart disease."

Because of garlic's known antithrombotic properties, doctors recommend caution in taking garlic supplements for patients already on an anticoagulant drug or who are taking daily aspirin. It is also recommended to stop taking high dosages of garlic 7 to 10 days before surgery because garlic can prolong bleeding time and has been associated (in one case report) with spontaneous spinal epidural hematoma.

Diabetes

Alternative medicine practitioners have long regarded garlic as useful to diabetics, not only for the cardiovascular reasons discussed above, but also for its ability to possibly lower blood sugar. It must be noted, though, that no major clinical trial has proven this claim. There have been studies done on lab animals, namely rats, that suggest garlic can improve blood glucose levels, but there are no conclusive results yet for humans.

But there is another reason for diabetics to be excited over garlic. A 2010 study, reported in the *Journal of Agricultural and Food Chemistry*, found that garlic has "significant" potential for preventing cardiomyopathy, a form of heart disease that is a leading cause of death in diabetics. The study, conducted on animals using garlic oil, showed a definite increased protection against heart damage, which scientists believe is due to the potent antioxidant properties of garlic oil. "In conclusion," the report notes, "garlic oil possesses significant potential for protecting hearts from diabetes-induced cardiomyopathy."

Cancer

One of the most exciting areas in which garlic is being studied is in the field of cancer research. Scientists have long known that there is an inverse relationship between rates of cancer and garlic intake. In northern China, for example, where consumption of garlic is as high as five to ten cloves a day, there is a markedly low incidence of stomach cancer. (Chinese men also have the lowest rate of prostate cancer in the world.) Similar observations have been made in Italy, Sweden, and the Netherlands, where lower rates of gastrointestinal cancers have been linked to a high ingestion of garlic.

Dr. John Milner of the National Cancer Institute has long studied garlic's effectiveness in the fight against cancer. In an overview of several studies published in the *Journal of Nutrition*, he went on record as saying, "Evidence continues to point to the anticancer properties of fresh garlic extracts, aged garlic, garlic oil, and a number of specific organosulfur compounds generated by processing garlic."

These cancer-fighting compounds are produced when cloves are chopped or crushed, as many people would normally do before cooking with garlic. But Milner warns that to keep those compounds effective, don't immediately toss the garlic into the pot. His research has shown that heating the garlic immediately after chopping inactivates a crucial enzyme in the chemical chain.

"Crush or chop the cloves, then let them sit for 10 or 15 minutes while you prepare other ingredients," advises Milner. "This will give the anticancer compounds a chance to form." Conveniently, pre-chopped garlic available in stores, as well as chopped garlic that has been stored in the freezer, was also found to contain active cancer-fighting compounds.

Detoxification

Increasingly in today's industrialized world, our bodies are exposed to an alarming number of pollutants. Of major concern are metals such as lead, mercury, cadmium, and cobalt. These potentially toxic materials are absorbed into our systems through polluted air and water, and by other means such as exposure to lead-based paints, mercury-filled dental fillings, and contaminated fish.

The good news is that garlic helps to detoxify heavy metals in the body. Several Japanese and British studies have confirmed that the sulfurous compounds in garlic protect liver cells from the damaging effects of carbon tetrachloride and the industrial solvent bromobenzene. Hawaiian dentist Dr. Samuel Wong claims to have successfully lowered the mercury levels in his dental patients through garlic therapy. And Dr. Benjamin Lau in his book *Garlic and You* claims that garlic has a nullifying effect on radiation.

Antioxidant Effects

Dr. Lau's claims of radiation protection from garlic may not be that far-fetched. Garlic is a known antioxidant, meaning it works to reduce the cellular damage to the body caused by free radicals. Free radicals are highly reactive molecules associated with aging, heart disease, cancer, and a host of other conditions. They are formed by, among other things, cigarette smoke, air pollution, unprotected sun exposure, and radiation. Antioxidants such as garlic neutralize free radicals and even, in some cases, destroy them.

Immunity

Garlic has long been regarded as an immune system booster due to its antibacterial, antiviral, and nutritive properties. Additionally, in recent studies it has also been shown to increase the production of white blood cells and interferons (proteins that fight pathogens such as viruses and tumors), both important elements of the body's immune system.

In the late 1980s and continuing through the 1990s, several studies were done with Kyolic Aged Garlic Extract in which it was found that aged garlic enhanced natural killer (NK) cell activity. NK cells are a component of the innate immune system that combine with cancer cells or cells infected with viruses and release toxic granules into the abnormal cells to kill them. The studies further showed that aged garlic extract was more effective than raw garlic for boosting natural killer cell actions.

Infection

Of all the many medicinal uses for garlic, one of the oldest is as an antibiotic. Apparently it's true that with age comes wisdom, because modern science has conclusively proven our ancestors' insistence that garlic heals. Study after study has shown that garlic contains antibacterial and antiviral properties that are effective against a broad span of germs, including fungus, intestinal parasites, yeast, and a plethora of additional gram-positive and gram-negative bacteria (two major classifications of bacteria).

Particularly encouraging are studies and anecdotal data that show garlic to be effective in instances where a resistance has been built against conventional antibiotics. In 2001 the BBC ran a story about a South African doctor who successfully treated infected babies and children with a carefully prepared garlic solution. The solution was found to be particularly useful in those children who had been on antibiotics for a long time and had developed a resistance, as well as with those who suffered from antibiotic side effects like oral thrush.

A recent study conducted with mice showed that garlic was able to inhibit a type of staph infection that has become increasingly resistant to antibiotics and is being seen more and more in hospitals. Not only is this type of staph infection a potential danger for health care workers, but is particularly dangerous to people with weakened immune systems. In the study, garlic extract was fed to the mice sixteen hours after they were infected with the staph pathogen. After twenty-four hours, the infection was found to be significantly decreased.

Most scientists studying garlic's antimicrobial properties believe that fresh and raw garlic is the best bet in fighting bacteria. This is because it is believed that allicin – garlic's powerful but unstable infection-fighting compound – is destroyed by heat. A 1999 Israeli study found that pure allicin exhibited a broad range of antibacterial activity, including defenses against strains of *E. coli* and *Candida albicans*, as well as some intestinal protozoan parasites such as *Giardia lamblia* and *Entamoeba histolytic*.

Most recently, researchers at Washington State University (WSU) in 2012 found that a compound in garlic is 100 times more effective than two popular conventional antibiotics at fighting the *Campylobacter* bacterium, one of the most common causes of intestinal illness. *Campylobacter* affects some 2.4 million Americans every year, causing diarrhea, cramping, abdominal pain, and fever. Most infections stem from eating raw or undercooked poultry or from foods that have been cross-contaminated from infected surfaces and utensils. What makes this bacterium so hard to fight is that it's protected by a slimy biofilm that makes it 1,000 times more resistant to antibiotics. But what the WSU researchers found is that the garlic-derived compound diallyl sulfide is able to easily penetrate that biofilm and kill bacterial cells. "Diallyl sulfide could make many foods safer to eat," says Barbara Rasco, a co-author on the study. "It can be used to clean food preparation surfaces and as a preservative in packaged foods like potato and pasta salads, coleslaw and deli meats."

If garlic is so effective at killing bacteria, the question begs asking, wouldn't it also kill the "good" bacteria in the gut needed for healthy intestinal functions? The good news is that studies have shown it takes ten times more garlic to kill *Lactobacillus* (good) than *E. coli* (bad). And unlike the case with conventional antibiotics, which often deplenish good gut flora, there has been no indication that harmful microorganisms develop a resistance to garlic.

Here's a recipe for a garlic-based antibacterial and antiviral drink. If you have an infection, try drinking several of these drinks or soups each day. If you're germ-free and want to stay that way, imbibe one a day.

4 cloves of garlic

2 tomatoes

1 lemon

Salt for taste (sea salt preferred)

Toss all the ingredients in a juicer or blender and mix to desired consistency. Add salt for taste. (*Courtesy of Kim Evans, NaturalNews.com*)

Side Effects

"Since garlic has the power to save from death, endure it though it gives bad breath."

–Robert I, Duke of Normandy

Garlic Breath

While the health benefits of eating garlic are all good, the social consequences are sometimes not. The most frequently complained-about side effect of garlic is, of course, garlic breath. Purported remedies include:

- Chewing on a sprig of fresh parsley or mint

- Chewing on fresh cilantro

- Chewing on a coffee bean

- Sipping lemonade (real, not sugar laden)

- Sucking on a lemon

- Sipping green or mint tea

- Drinking milk with your meal (whole milk works best)

Garlic Hands

To remove the garlic smell from your hands, try these recommendations:

- Coffee grounds

- Baking soda and water paste

- Lemon juice and salt

- Stainless steel (Under running water, rub your hands on the sink, the faucet, a spoon – anything stainless steel. Finish by washing with soap and water. It works!)

Indigestion and Intolerance

Raw garlic is a very powerful substance. Consequently, many people experience mild to serious indigestion, heartburn, and/or flatulence when ingesting it in large quantities. Continual ingestion of large amounts of raw garlic could even cause damage to the digestive tract. Some unfortunate individuals have an actual garlic allergy that can result in stomach problems, a skin rash, headache, and fever. Others, while not truly allergic, are still garlic-sensitive to the point of exhibiting similar symptoms after eating a large amount of raw garlic. And finally, everyone should be heedful of keeping raw garlic in prolonged contact with the skin: it can and will cause blistering. If you're new to the wonderful world of garlic, you may want to take it slow and see just how much your system can handle a little at a time.

Medical Side Effects

Garlic is a strong substance that contains many active chemical compounds, some of which may interact or interfere with other drugs. If you plan on ingesting large amounts of garlic for health reasons, and you're currently on medication, it's best to check with your doctor first. It is known, for example, that garlic has blood thinning properties, and for this reason is recommended that people stop taking it seven to ten days before surgery or before giving birth. It may also not be the best substance to take in large quantities if you're already on an aspirin regime, take anticoagulants, blood pressure medication, or are on diabetes medication. If unsure, ask your doctor first.

Garlic Folk Remedies

"Oh, that miracle clove! Not only does garlic taste good, it cures baldness and tennis elbow, too."

–Laurie Burrows Grad

Throughout the ages and across a vast expanse of cultures and traditions ranging from Ayurvedic to Americana, garlic has been used as a health-promoting and healing plant. Some of the claims regarding garlic's prowess could justifiably raise an eyebrow or two. (Baldness? Tennis elbow?)

Remarkably, though, there are numerous old world recommendations for garlic that new world science has corroborated. The ancient Egyptians, for example, prescribed garlic as a heart medicine. As shown in the previous chapter, numerous modern studies have confirmed that garlic does indeed benefit the heart and circulatory system. The ancient Greeks and Romans used garlic as protection against toxins and infections. Again, contemporary research has overwhelmingly proven garlic's antibacterial and antiviral properties. In the Far East, too, garlic has been long revered for its medicinal as well as culinary benefits. Ancient texts in China, Japan, and India describe garlic as being useful for everything from preserving food to improving male potency.

The folk remedies listed below are for your personal review and discernment. Though not all of them have been put to the test in a modern laboratory, that doesn't mean they're without merit. Researchers have just begun to peel the very tip of the garlic bulb, so to speak, in terms of validating the efficacy of garlic. As Dr. Richard Rivlin reminds us in his journal article "Historical Perspective on the

Use of Garlic": "Folk wisdom should not be ignored because it may teach us valuable lessons." So read and reap with an open mind the following wisdom from the ages. You just may be surprised at how wise those "old folks" actually were.

Acne

Crush or puree a clove of garlic. Using a cotton ball or your fingers, rub the affected area with the garlic. Let it sit for about 10 minutes before washing off with water. Your skin won't smell all that good, but the antibacterial and antifungal properties of garlic will help clear up the outbreaks, even those deep acne cysts that don't always respond to other treatments.

Arthritis

On a daily basis, eat plenty of garlic in addition to drinking one tablespoon of apple cider vinegar and one teaspoon of honey in a cup of warm water.

Asthma

St. Hildegard recommended drinking a garlic tea made by simmering three cloves of garlic in water for twenty minutes, straining then sipping.

Ayurvedic medicine prescribes boiling three cloves of garlic in milk and eating every night.

Western folk medicine recommends mixing together two peeled and chopped cloves of garlic with a teaspoon of apple cider vinegar and a teaspoon of honey, and eating this in the morning on an empty stomach.

Athlete's Foot

Soak a washcloth in vinegar, rub garlic juice on the cloth, and then use the cloth to soak/wash the affected area. Rinse the foot with water afterwards. The fungus should clear up in about a week.

Squeeze the juice from a broken clove of garlic on the afflicted area.

Place freshly crushed garlic on the fungus for a half-hour. Rinse off with water.

Dust your feet daily with garlic powder.

*[**Note:** If the skin is broken, garlic will burn that area. Though not harmful, it is painful, so caution is advised.]*

Colds and Flu

Make a virus-fighting elixir by placing several cloves of garlic in a blender along with one-third cup of olive oil. Blend until smooth. Take a teaspoon of the mix every hour or two. Keep the mixture refrigerated, and throw it away after two to three days.

Drink steaming hot chicken soup seasoned with garlic.

Cold Sores

Cut a garlic clove in half and place it directly on the cold sore for 10 minutes, several times a day. The acidity may cause a bit of initial discomfort.

Digestion

Add cooked and raw garlic to your daily diet, say many herbalists and naturopaths, to aid digestion, cure diarrhea, and ease constipation. Ayurvedic medicine prescribes it because it supposedly stimulates intestinal movement and the secretion of digestive juices.

Earache

Crush a clove of garlic and place it in a teaspoon of hot olive oil for five minutes. Strain, let cool, then drip a few drops into your ear canal. You can also purchase garlic oil made for this purpose at natural health food stores. Alternatively, pierce a garlic oil capsule and drizzle a few drops into the afflicted ear.

Psoriasis

The persistent tightness and itching caused by psoriasis can be eased or even prevented by garlic's anti-inflammatory properties. Active compounds in garlic interact with arachidonic acid, an omega fatty acid in the skin linked to psoriasis. Rub garlic oil directly on affected areas once or twice a day.

Ringworm

Mix pressed garlic with a small amount of sesame oil and apply to the affected area three times a day.

Sore Throat

Gargle with hot water mixed with garlic juice.

Sip this garlic-ginger tea: Add 2 cloves of slightly crushed garlic and 2 to 3 slices of ginger to a pan of water (approximately 1 cup). Cover the pan and allow mixture to steep for about 10 minutes. Then warm slightly, strain the liquid, and drink.

Splinters

Cut a thin slice off a garlic clove, place it on the afflicted area, and secure with a bandage or tape. Leave on for several hours or overnight. The combination of garlic and adhesive should draw the splinter (or shard of glass) to the surface for easy removal. Garlic's antibacterial properties will also help keep out infection and soreness.

Toothache

An old Russian folk remedy prescribes pressing raw garlic on the inside of the wrist that is opposite your sore tooth. (e.g., left wrist for a right side tooth). Leave the garlic on for about 20 minutes.

Apply a cut clove of garlic directly on the sore tooth for about 40 minutes.

Warts

Rub with fresh mashed garlic.

Weight Loss

Daily ingestion of garlic may help with weight loss efforts by acting as a natural appetite suppressant. The strong odor of garlic as well as the active compounds in the garlic itself stimulate the satiety center in the brain, reducing feelings of hunger. Garlic is also said to increase the brain's sensitivity to leptin, a hormone that helps regulate appetite. Garlic also increases the metabolism. A higher metabolism burns calories faster and can lead to weight loss.

Yeast Infections

Include more raw garlic in your daily diet if you have a yeast infection or are prone to them. Many herbalists recommend eating a full clove, which can be chewed and washed down with a glass of water for a quick daily treatment.

If chewing raw garlic doesn't appeal to you, finely mince it and then add it to water or juice and swallow quickly.

Zinc Deficiency

Approximately 30 percent of the world's population suffers from a zinc deficiency. Garlic not only contains a rich amount of zinc itself, but a 2010 study found that adding garlic (and onions) to both cooked and raw cereals and other grains increased zinc absorption up to 160 percent.

Thinking Outside the Bulb

Unusual Uses For Garlic

"Each clove of garlic has a sacred power."
–Rev. Hilderic Friend

Aphrodisiac

The ancient Greeks, Romans, Indians, and Jews can't all be wrong. Garlic has long been suspected of revving romantic motors due to its efficacy in aiding circulation and thus pumping blood to the, eh, extremities.

Face Cleanser

Make a paste of minced garlic, 2 teaspoons of olive oil, and 1 tablespoon of honey. Apply evenly to skin using circular, massaging motions. Leave on for 20 minutes, then rinse with warm water. This is said to tighten and exfoliate the skin. (Be careful if you have open wounds or blistering pimples, as the garlic will burn.)

Fingernail Health

Rub cloves of garlic on your fingernails and let sit for a bit before rinsing to strengthen them.

Fish Bait

While garlic might deter insects, it has the opposite effect on fish. Put a bunch of small marshmallows in a bowl of garlic powder or crushed garlic and roll them around until they're well covered. Use the marshmallows as bait for catfish, carp, trout, bass, and other fish.

Flea Deterrent

Grate a small amount of fresh garlic onto your dog's food, but don't overdo it, as it could be harmful in large amounts. Some pet owners swear it's also good for deterring ticks and other parasites. Alternatively, check the pet store for garlic and brewers yeast capsules, which when taken orally discourage fleas from biting.

Glass Repair

Crush a clove of garlic and rub the sticky, viscous juice into the cracks and wipe away the excess. While this won't be effective for major jobs, it can be used to fill in hairline cracks in glass and hold them together.

Mosquito Repellent

Ward off the little vampires by placing cloves of garlic around your patio sitting area in the evening. For a more hardcore approach, apply garlic oil/juice on your exposed skin.

Pesticide #1

In a blender, puree **6-8 cloves of garlic, 3-5 hot chile peppers**, and **3 cups of water**. Let stand overnight (or at least 2 hours), then strain the mixture through a piece of cheesecloth or coffee filter to get rid of the particles that could clog up a sprayer. Pour the strained mixture into a container with a plastic lid, add **1 tablespoon of liquid castile soap**, and stir thoroughly. This is a concentrated substance, so use about 3 tablespoons in a small spray bottle filled with water and apply to your plants. Repeat the applications as needed.

Pesticide #2

Mince **3 garlic cloves** and let them sit in **2 tablespoons of mineral oil** for 24 hours. Then strain out the garlic and add the oil, along with **1 teaspoon of liquid dish soap**, to **1 pint of water** in a spray bottle. Spray on infested plants during the cool part of the day.

Pesticide #3

If you want all the planet-protecting power and goodness of a garlic-based insect repellent, but don't want the hassle of making your own, consider buying Garlic Barrier, a strong liquid garlic extract that mixes with water for spraying on farm and garden plants.

Garlic Fun Facts

*"A nickel will get you on the subway, but garlic will get you
a seat."*

−Yiddish Proverb

Garlic was known by the ancient Romans as the "vegetable of Mars" (the god of war).

At ancient Greek and Roman marriages the brides carried bouquets of garlic and other herbs instead of flowers.

Ancient Jewish scribe Ezra recommended eating garlic on Friday nights, which in Hebrew tradition is the night for marital intimacy.

The Egyptians used to swear on cloves of garlic before taking an oath in the same way we swear on the Bible today.

Tutankhamen was sent into the afterlife with garlic at his side.

When King Henry IV was born, it is rumored that garlic was rubbed on his lips to protect him from demons and witches.

Legend has it that Tibetan monks were forbidden from entering monasteries if they had eaten garlic because of its reputation for arousing sexual desire.

In the Middle Ages, garlic was hung in braided strands across the entrances of houses to prevent evil spirits from entering.

Garlic is mentioned 21 times in Bram Stoker's Dracula but only four times in all of Shakespeare.

Garlic attracts leeches. They take 14.9 seconds to attach to a hand covered with garlic but 44.9 seconds to suck blood from a clean one.

Chicago was named after the American Indian word for the wild garlic that grew around Lake Michigan, *chicagaoua*.

American Indians would spread wild garlic cloves on the ground for the birds and when the birds ate it, they would weaken, thus making them easier to catch.

The "wild garlic" of Native American lore is not actual garlic (*Allium sativum*), but is a related plant from the garlic genus *Allium*. It is more or less considered a nuisance weed by gardeners today.

There are over 300 varieties of garlic grown all over the world.

China is the world's largest garlic producer, having produced 30 *billion* pounds of the stuff in 2010.

Garlic: Top 6 Producing Countries		(USDA)
	2000	2010
World Total	24.45 billion lbs	38.88 billion lbs
China	16.5 billion lbs	30.06 billion lbs
India	1.16 billion lbs	1.83 billion lbs
South Korea	1.05 billion lbs	600 million lbs
Egypt	590 million lbs	540 million lbs
Russia	430 million lbs	470 million lbs
United States	560 million lbs	370 million lbs

California produces more than 250 million pounds of garlic each year.

The Gilroy Garlic Festival (Gilroy, California) is held in July each year.

Garlic only contains 4 calories per clove.

The fear of garlic is known as alliumphobia.

National Garlic Day is April 19.

Garlic Quotes

"Shallots are for babies; onions are for men; garlic is for heroes."
　　　–Author unknown

"What garlic is to food, insanity is to art."
　　　–Augustus Saint-Gaudens

"Most dear actors, eat no onions nor garlic, for we are to utter sweet breath."
　　　–William Shakespeare, *A Midsummer Night's Dream*

"Garlick maketh a man wynke, drynke, and stynke."
　　　–Thomas Nash

"Tomatoes and oregano make it Italian; wine and tarragon make it French; sour cream makes it Russian; lemon and cinnamon make it Greek; soy sauce makes it Chinese; garlic makes it good."
　　　–Alice May Brock (of Alice's Restaurant)

"Vulgarity is the garlic in the salad of life."
　　　–Cyril Connolly

"A garlic caress is stimulating. A garlic excess soporific."
　　　–Curnonsky

"There's no doubt that after you eat a lot of garlic, you just kind of feel like you are floating, you feel ultra-confident, you feel capable of going out and whipping your weight in wild cats."

–Les Blank

"Without garlic, I simply would not care to live."

–Louis Diat, Chef of the Ritz Hotel (1885-1958)

"Do not eat garlic or onions; for their smell will reveal that you are a peasant."

–Cervantes, *Don Quixote*

"Garlic used as it should be used is the soul, the divine essence, of cookery. The cook who can employ it successfully will be found to possess the delicacy of perception, the accuracy of judgment, and the dexterity of hand which go to the formation of a great artist."

–Mrs. W. G. Waters

"No one is indifferent to garlic. People either love it or hate it, and most good cooks seem to belong in the first group."

–Faye Levy

"The air of Provence was particularly perfumed by the refined essence of this mystically attractive bulb."

–Alexandre Dumas

"The only advice I can give to aspiring writers is don't do it unless you're willing to give your whole life to it. Red wine and garlic also helps."

–Jim Harrison

"What do you think? Young women of rank eat – you will never guess what – garlick!"

–Percy Bysshe Shelley

"The best thing to do with garlic of course, is to eat it."

–Sylvia Rubin

"We remember the fish, which we did eat in Egypt freely; the cucumbers, and the melons, and the leeks, and the onions, and the garlic."

–*The Holy Bible*, Numbers 11

"Since garlic then hath powers to save from death, bear with it though it makes unsavory breath."

–Salerno Regimen of Health (12th century)

"It is not really an exaggeration to say that peace and happiness begin, geographically, where garlic is used in cooking."

–X. Marcel Boulestin, first television chef (1878-1943)

"Stop and smell the garlic! That's all you have to do."

–William Shatner

"You're a monster, Mr. Grinch, Your heart's an empty hole, Your brain is full of spiders, You've got garlic in your soul, Mr. Grinch."

–Dr. Seuss

"You can never have enough garlic. With enough garlic, you can eat *The New York Times*."

–Morley Safer

Garlic Resources on the Web

The Garlic Store
www.thegarlicstore.com

Garlic World
www.garlicworld.com

Christopher Ranch
www.christopherranch.com

Gourmet Garlic Gardens
gourmetgarlicgardens.com

Gilroy Garlic Festival
gilroygarlicfestival.com

Boundary Garlic
www.garlicfarm.ca

Hood River Garlic
www.hoodrivergarlic.com

Filaree Garlic Farm
www.filareefarm.com

The Garlic Farm (U.K.)
www.thegarlicfarm.co.uk

Kyolic Aged Garlic Extract
www.kyolic.com

Garlic Barrier Insect Repellent
www.garlicbarrier.com

Selected References

American Chemical Society. "Garlic Oil Shows Protective Effect Against Heart Disease in Diabetes." *ScienceDaily.com*, 1 Oct. 2010.

Bader, Myles. *2001 Food Secrets Revealed.* Las Vegas, NV: Northstar Publishing, 1997.

Beare, Sally. *50 Secrets of the World's Longest Living People.* New York: Marlowe & Co, 2006.

Bowden, Jonny. *The 150 Healthiest Foods on Earth: The Surprising, Unbiased Truth About What You Should Eat and Why.* Gloucester, MA: Fair Winds Press, 2007.

Corderoy, Amy. "Garlic Cuts High Blood Pressure." *The Age*, 9 January 2013.

Hornick, Betsy, and Eric Yarnell. "Medical Uses for Garlic." *DiscoveryHealth.com*, 21 March 2006.

Editors of Publications International, Ltd.. "Garlic." 19 March 2007. *HowStuffWorks.com.*

Huber, Gary. "The Medicinal Use of Garlic in History." *AmazingHerbs.com.*

Institute of Food Technologists (IFT). "Drinking Milk Can Prevent Garlic Breath, Study Finds." *ScienceDaily.com*, 4 Feb. 2013.

Koch, Heinrich P., and Larry D. Lawson. *Garlic: The Science and Therapeutic Application of Allium Sativum L. and Related Species.* Baltimore: Williams & Wilkins, 1996.

Lau, Benjamin, M.D. *Garlic and You: The Modern Medicine*. Denver, CO: Apple Tree Publishing, 1999.

Lie, Sarah. *Ayurveda*. Blacklick, OH: McGraw-Hill Companies, 2007.

Los Angeles Biomedical Research Institute at Harbor-UCLA Medical Center (LA BioMed). "New Study Shows Aged Garlic Extract Can Reduce Dangerous Plaque Buildup in Arteries: Supplement Can Help Prevent Progression of Heart Disease." *ScienceDaily.com*, 21 January 2016.

Meredith, Ted Jordan. *The Complete Book of Garlic: A Guide for Gardeners, Growers, and Serious Cooks*. Portland, OR: Timber Press, 2008.

Meyers, Michele. *Garlic: An Herb Society of America Guide*. Kirtland, OH: The Herb Society of America, 2006.

Milner, John A. "Preclinical Perspectives on Garlic and Cancer." *Journal of Nutrition*, March 2006, Vol. 136, No. 3 827S-831S.

Pacchioli, David. "The Joy of Garlic." *Research/Penn State*, Vol. 20, No. 2, 1999.

Petrovska, B., & Cekovska, S. (2010). "Extracts From the History and Medical Properties of Garlic." *Pharmacognosy Reviews*, 10 July 2010.

Powell, Julie. "The Extraordinary Heart Health Benefits of Aged Garlic Extract—An Interview with Dr. Matthew Budoff." *LivingNaturally.com*.

Pratt, Steven, and Kathy Matthews. *Superfoods Healthstyle: Simple Changes to Get the Most Out of Life for the Rest of Your Life*. New York: Harper, 2007.

Renoux, Victoria. *For the Love of Garlic: The Complete Guide to Garlic Cuisine*. Garden City Park, NY: Square One Publishers, 2005.

Rivlin, RS. "Historical Perspective on the Use of Garlic." *The Journal of Nutrition*, 1 March 2001.

Shulman, Martha Rose. *Garlic Cookery*. New York: Thorsons Publishers, 1984.

Tattelman, Ellen, M.D. "Health Effects of Garlic." *American Family Physician*, 1 July 2005.

Thacker, Emily. *The Garlic Book*. Canton, OH: Tresco Publishers, 1994.

Tweed, V. (2010). *Garlic: Myth, Magic, or Fact?* Better Nutrition, November 2010.

Washington State University. "Garlic Compound Fights Source of Food-Borne Illness Better Than Antibiotics." *ScienceDaily.com*, 1 May 2012.

White, Martha. *Traditional Home Remedies*. London: Time-Life, 2000.

About the Author

M.B. Ryther is a freelance writer whose work has appeared in a variety of print and online magazines, including *Country Woman*, *Mother Earth News*, *Woman's World*, *Catholic Digest*, *L.A. Parent*, and *Boys' Life*. She lives in eastern Washington with her husband and children.